DATE DUE

DISCARD

NOV 2 1 2007		
SEP 1 8 2008		
FEB 2 6 2010		
JUN 1 7 2011		
JUL 2 0 2011 MAR 1 9 2013		
APR 2 9 2013		
SEP 2 2 2014		

DISCARD

A Greedy Little Pig

Written by Charnan Simon • Illustrated by Marcy Ramsey

Published in the United States of America by The Child's World®
PO Box 326 • Chanhassen, MN 55317-0326
800-599-READ • www.childsworld.com

Reading Adviser

Cecilia Minden-Cupp, PhD, Former Language and Literacy Program Director,
Harvard Graduate School of Education, Cambridge, Massachusetts

Acknowledgments

The Child's World®: Mary Berendes, Publishing Director

Editorial Directions, Inc.: E. Russell Primm, Editorial Director and Project Manager;
Katie Marsico, Associate Editor; Judith Shiffer, Assistant Editor; Caroline Wood, Editorial Assistant

The Design Lab: Kathleen Petelinsek, Design and Art Production

Library of Congress Cataloging-in-Publication Data

Simon, Charnan.
  A greedy little pig / written by Charnan Simon ; illustrated by Marcy Ramsey.
    p. cm. — (Magic door to learning)
  Summary: Sammie Swine learns that being greedy has consequences.
  ISBN 1-59296-622-5 (library bound : alk. paper)
  [1. Greed—Fiction. 2. Behavior—Fiction. 3. Pigs—Fiction.] I. Ramsey, Marcy Dunn, ill.
II. Title. III. Series.
  PZ7.S6035Gre 2006
  [E]—dc22   2006001406

A book is a door, a magic door.
It can take you places
you have never been before.
Ready? Set?
Turn the page.
Open the door.
Now it is time to explore.

Sammie Swine was a greedy little pig.

5

"I'll take that!" Sammie told his friend Freddy. Then he shoved the whole watermelon in his mouth.

"Give me some!"
Sammie told his
friend Babe. Then
he gobbled up every
single ear of corn.

9

"Yum!" Sammie told his friend Wilbur.

Then he slurped down Wilbur's
milkshake—as well as his own.

One day, Sammie and
his friends went to the fair.

It was great! There
was so much to see
and so much to eat!

Sammie loaded up
on cotton candy
and popcorn balls
and caramel apples.

He grabbed ice-cream
cones and root beer floats
and lemon-lime slushies.
He used up every bit of
mustard on his veggie
dogs. "Ahhh," Sammie
sighed, as he bit into a
bun. "This is the life!"

"AHHHHHH!" Sammie
cried. The hot mustard
on his veggie dogs had
bitten him back!

"Ouch, ouch, ouch, ouch, OUCH!
Too much! Too hot! Oh, help!"

20

Freddy and Babe and Wilbur looked at Sammie. They looked at each other. Then Freddy gave Sammie a snow cone. Babe patted Sammie on the back. Wilbur handed Sammie a napkin. "Sammie," they said. "You are a greedy little pig."

Now Sammie isn't so greedy.
He tries to be a generous
little pig. But it isn't always
easy! Luckily, Freddy and
Babe and Wilbur are always
around to help.

Our story is over, but there is still much to explore beyond the magic door!

Do you enjoy trying new foods? It's fun to sample a little bit of a lot of exciting, new dishes. With an adult's help, plan a special picnic with as many friends as you can. Ask each friend to bring a different food. This way, everyone gets to taste more than one treat without acting greedy or getting too full.

These books will help you explore at the library and at home:

Falconer, Ian. *Olivia Saves the Circus.* New York: Atheneum Books for Young Readers, 2001.

Numeroff, Laura, and Felicia Bond (illustrator). *If You Give a Pig a Party.* New York: Laura Geringer Books, 2005.

About the Author

Charnan Simon lives in Madison, Wisconsin, where she can usually be found sitting at her desk and writing books, unless she is sitting at her desk and looking out the window. Charnan has one husband, two daughters, and two very helpful cats.

About the Illustrator

Marcy Ramsey has always been an artist in some way, shape, or form, and has experience in graphic design, portraiture, printmaking, teaching, painting, and illustrating. It's like breathing for her, and she has a hard time explaining anything without a pencil.